it's ok but it leaves a nasty taste in your mouse

SPOT THE AUTHOR

Drawings and Verses
by Simon Drew

ANTIQUE COLLECTORS' CLUB

to
caroline

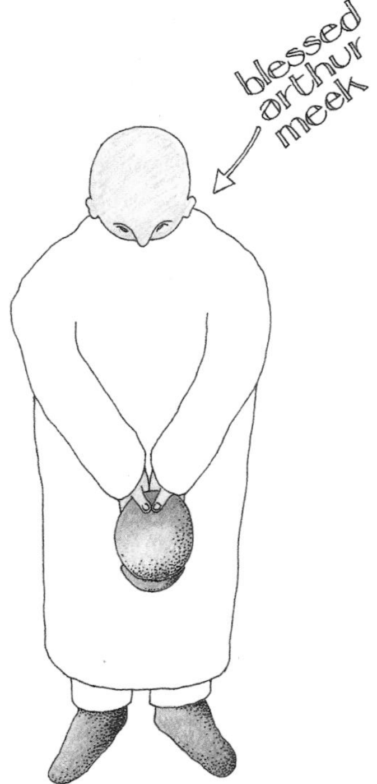

ISBN 1 85149 453 7

British Library Cataloguing-in-Publication Data
A catalogue record for this book is available from the British Library

Published by the Antique Collectors' Club Ltd., Sandy Lane, Old Martlesham, Woodbridge, Suffolk IP12 4SD
Printed and bound in Spain

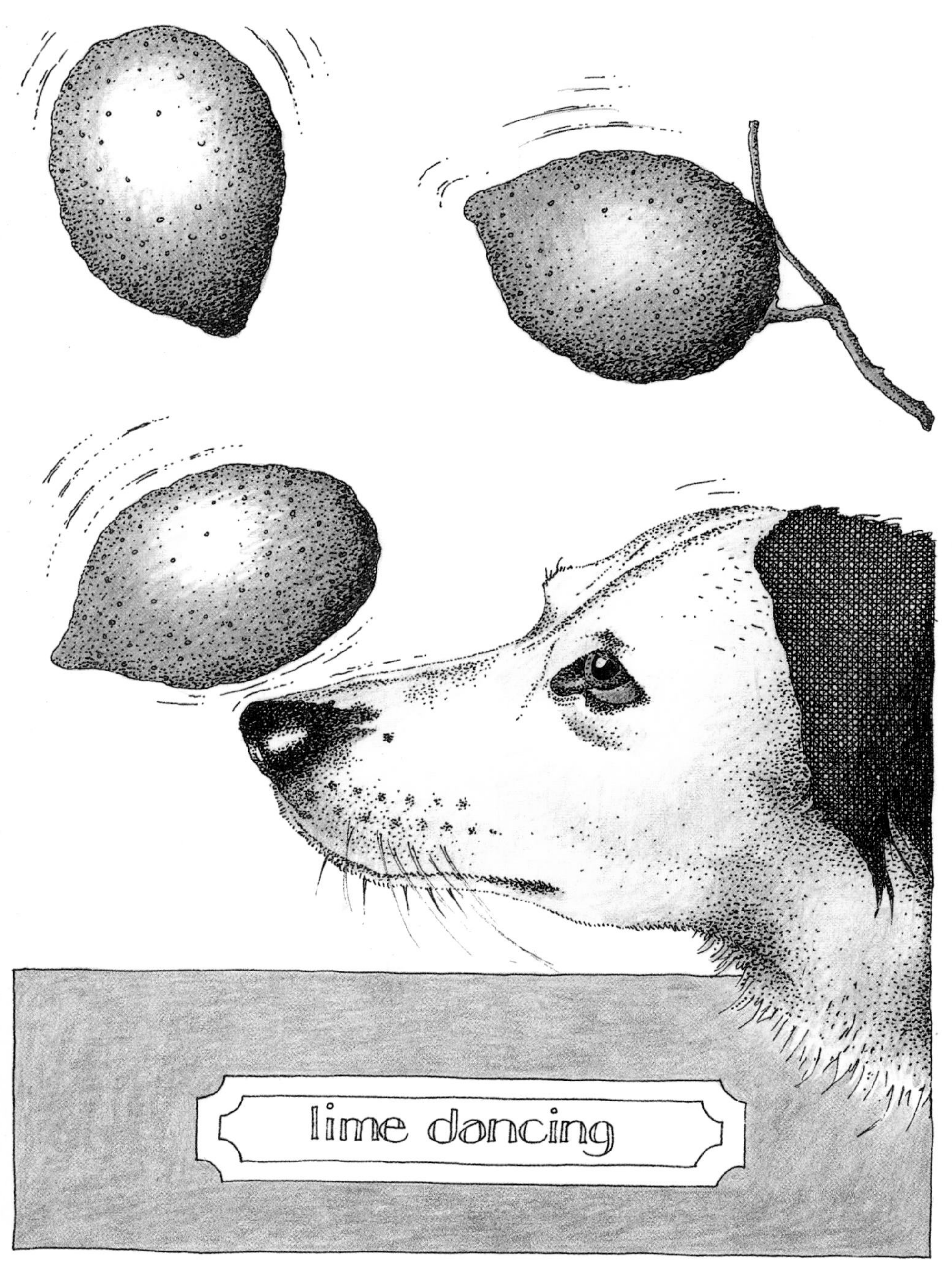
lime dancing

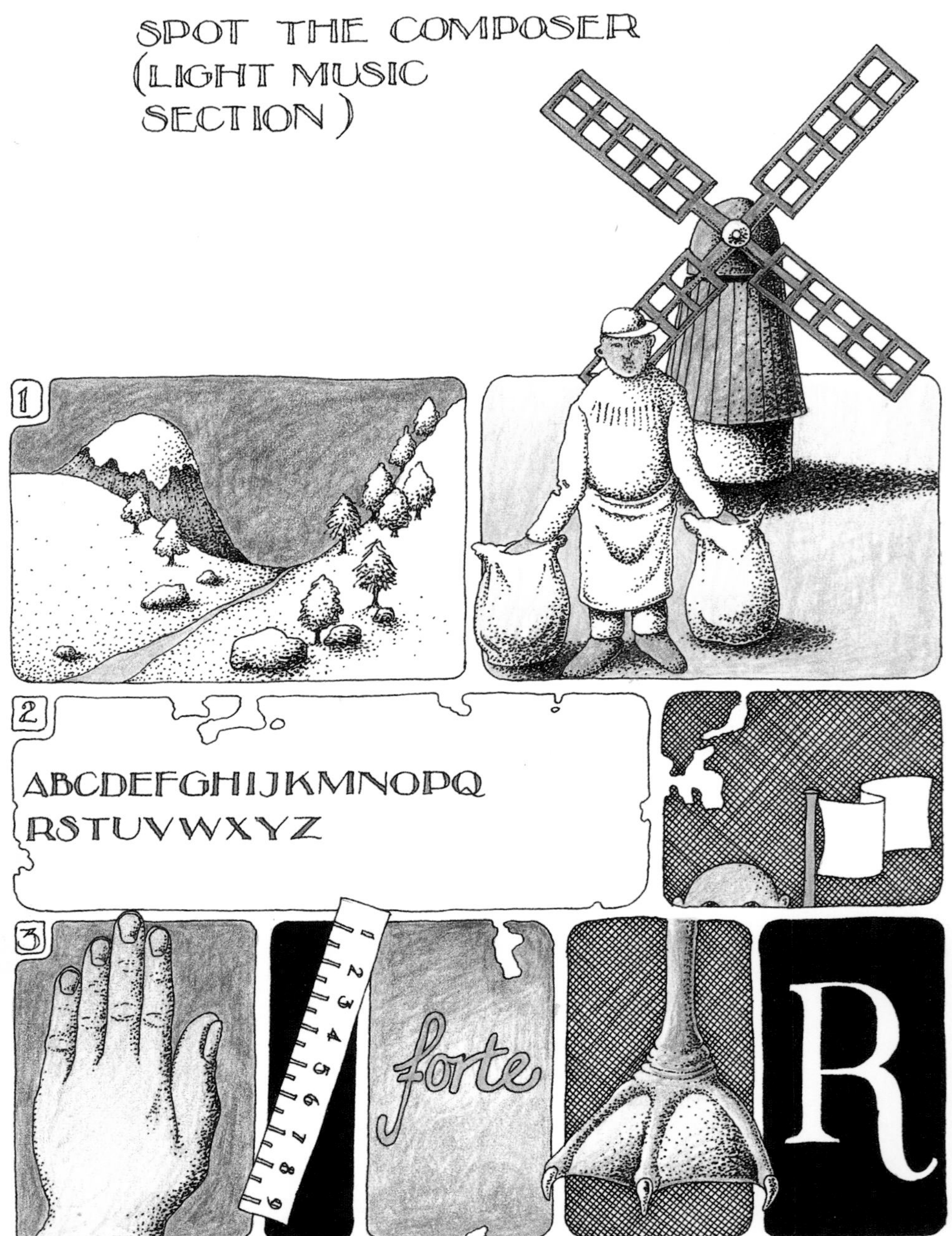
SPOT THE COMPOSER (LIGHT MUSIC SECTION)
1
2
ABCDEFGHIJKMNOPQ
RSTUVWXYZ
3
1 2 3 4 5 6 7 8 9
forte
R

SPOT THE COMPOSER

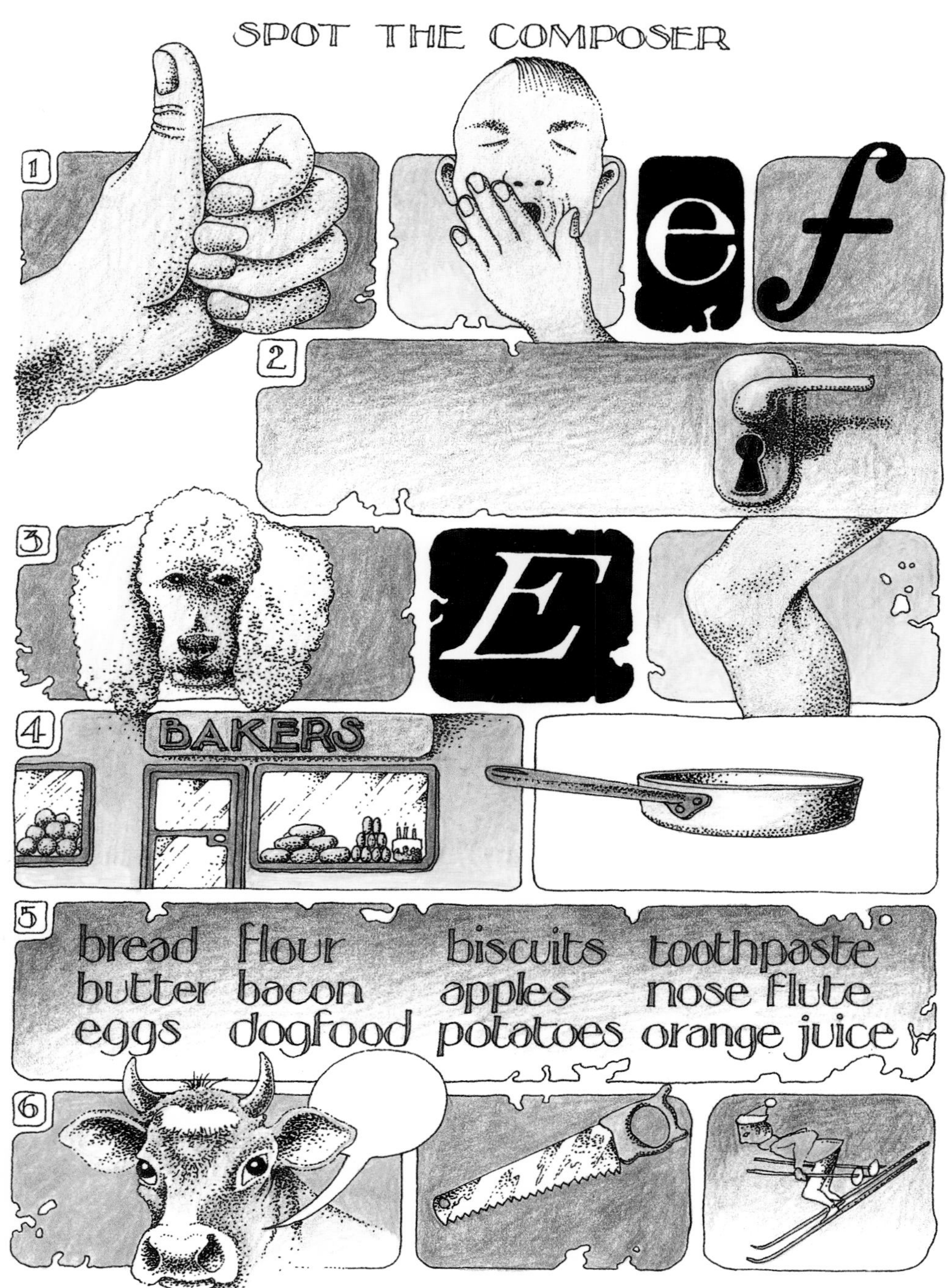

When you're young and you go to your mother
and you think that you want to annoy her,
tell her you might turn to crime;
or worse....that you might be a lawyer.

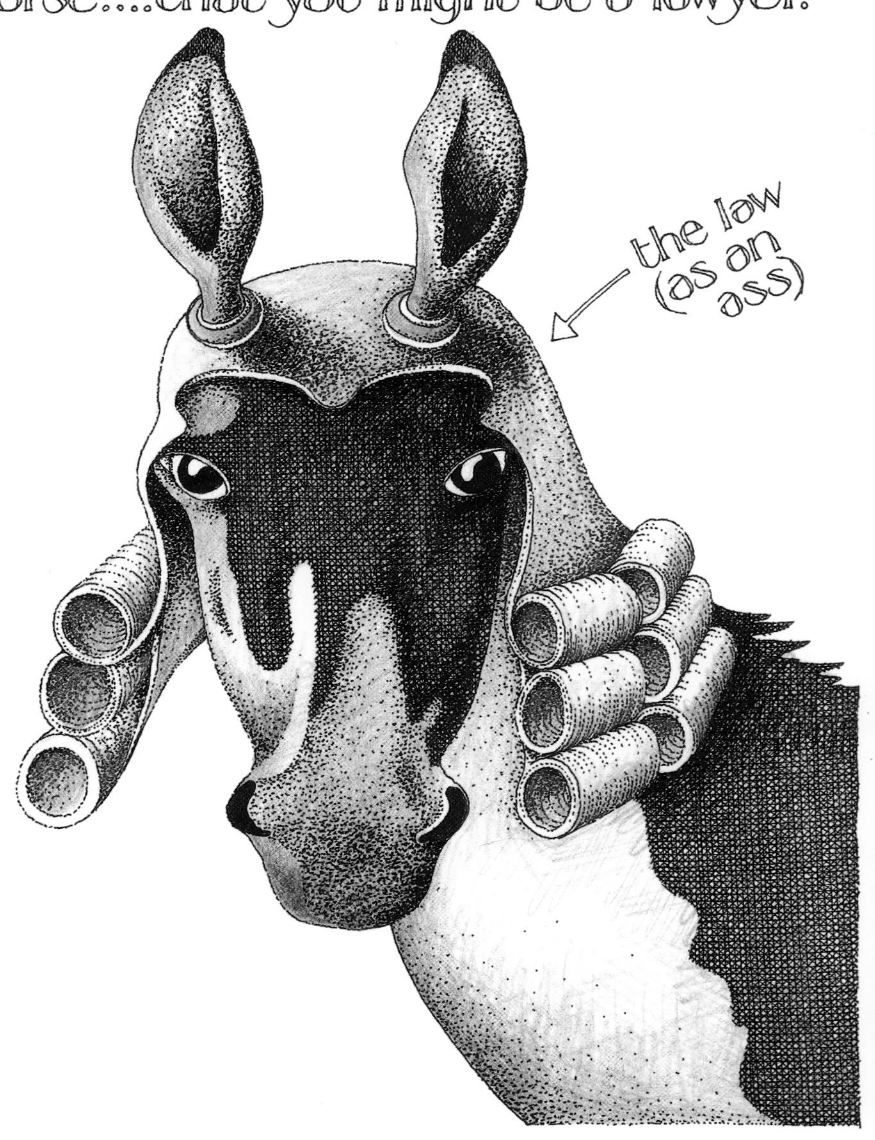

situations to avoid . . . . . .

golf war syndrome

mole voice choir

chariots of fur

sitting duck

SPOT THE CHRISTMAS SONG

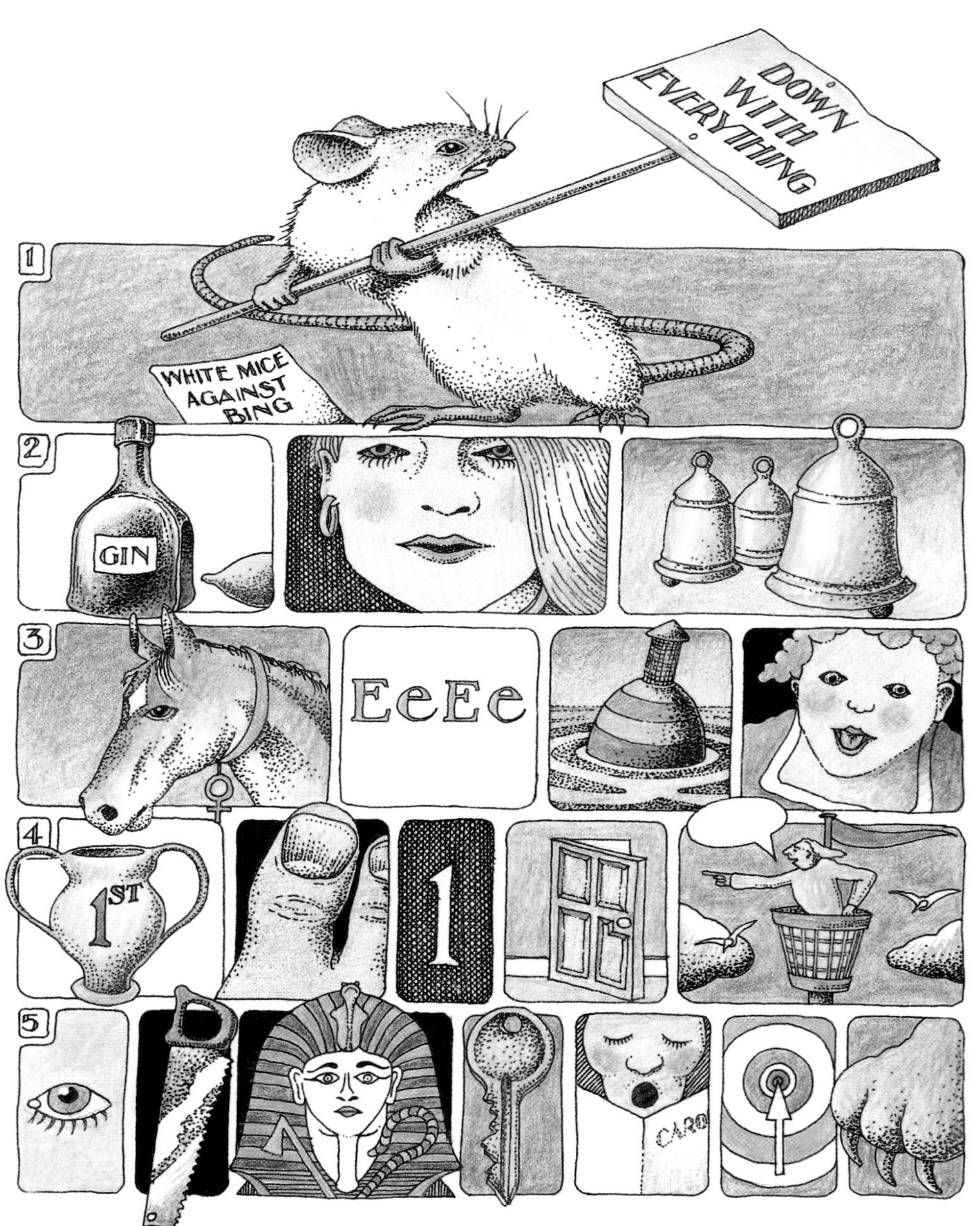

SPOT THE MUSICAL INSTRUMENTS

It took Edward
twenty years of playing golf
to find the perfect swing.

the joy of sets

SPOT THE PROFESSION

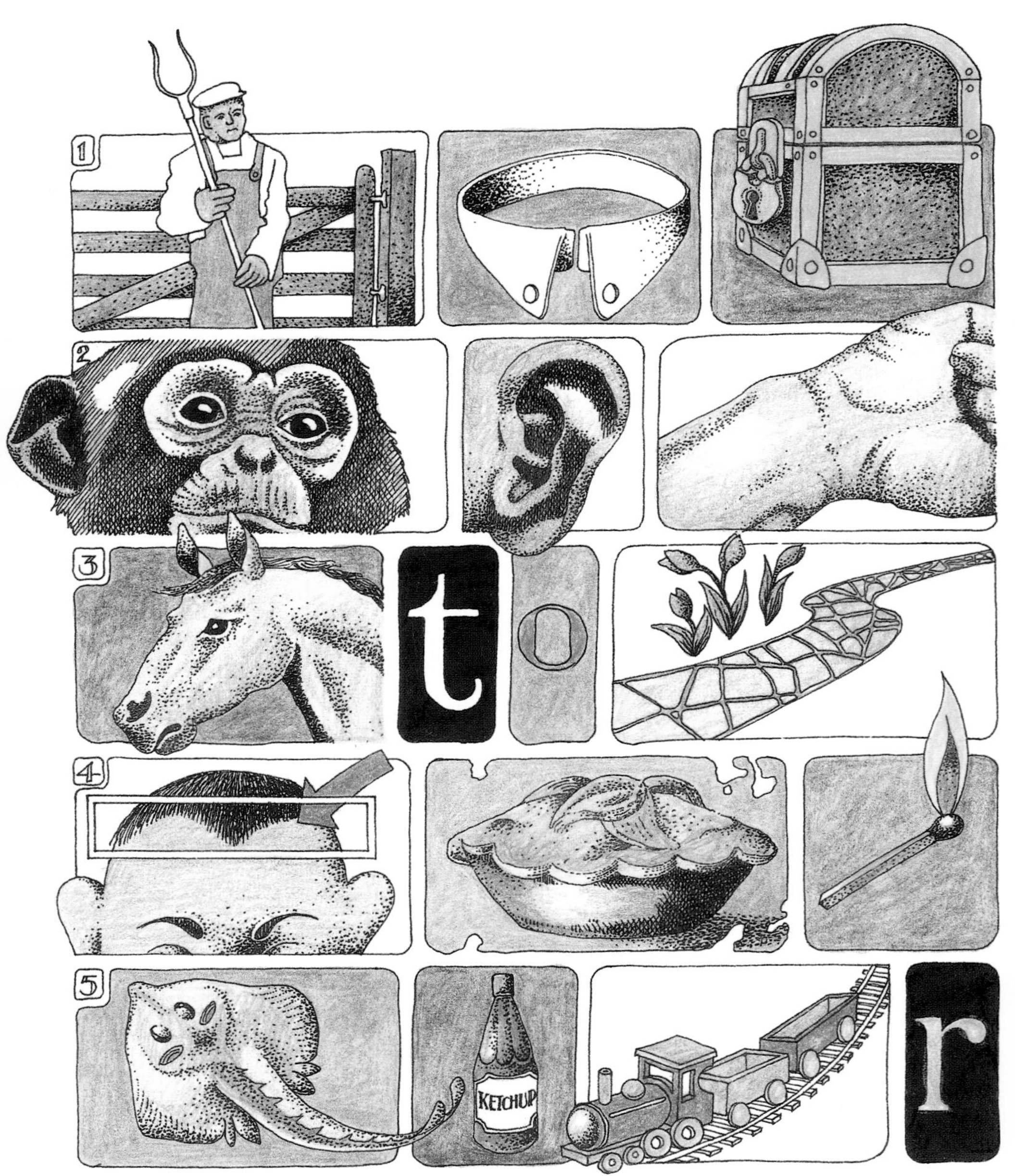

SPOT THE PLAY

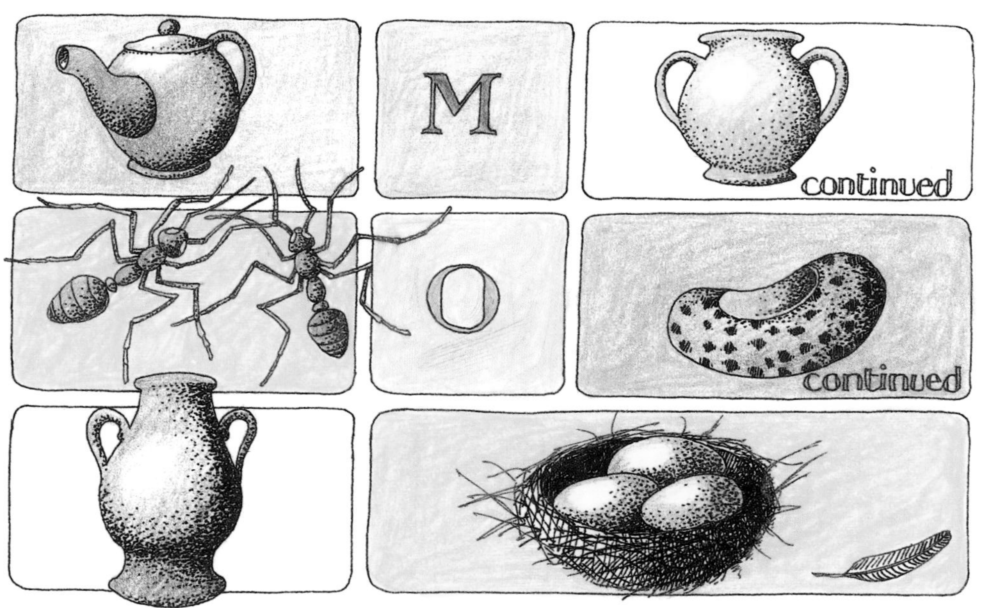

gladys knight and the popes

receding hare

SPOT THE COUNTRY

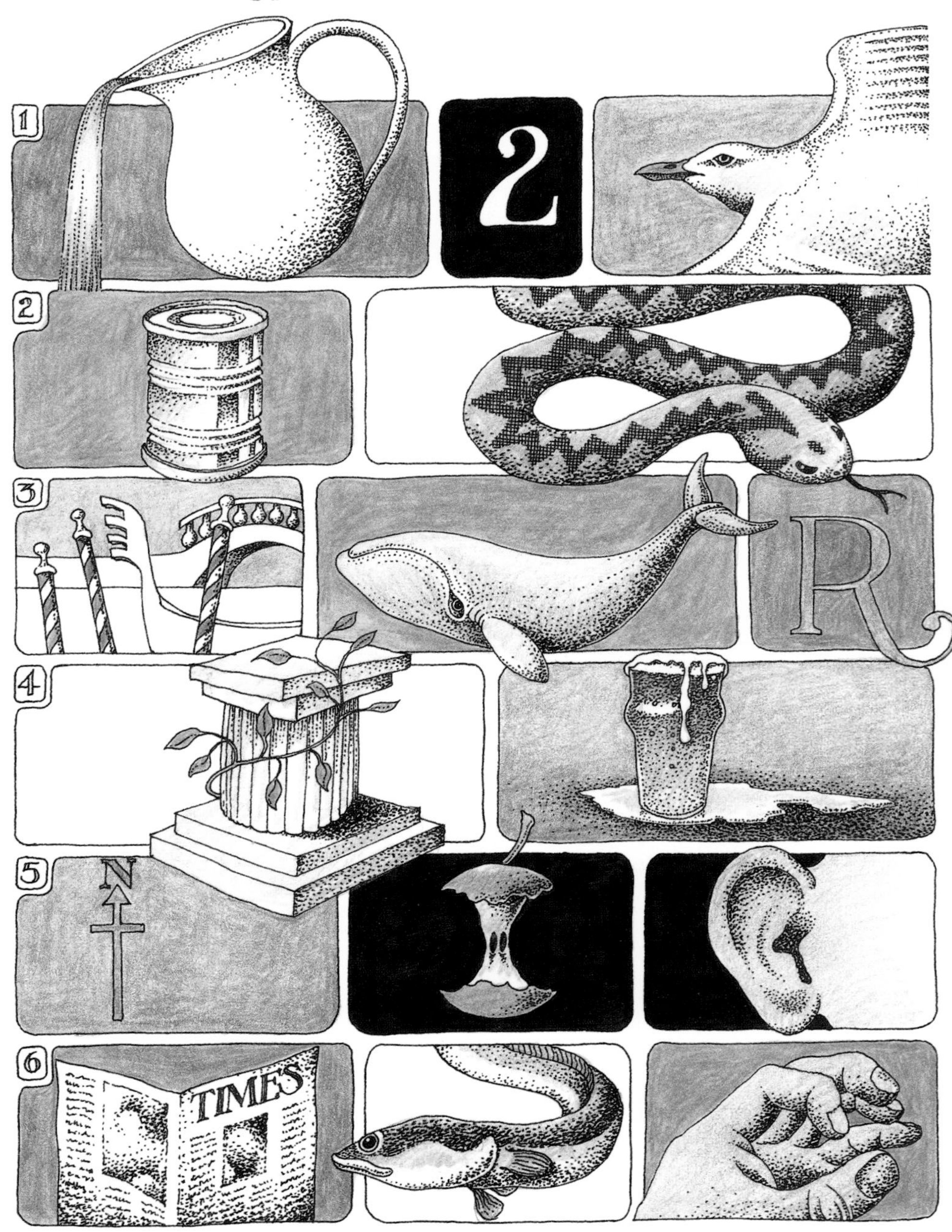

SPOT ANOTHER SHAKESPEARE PLAY

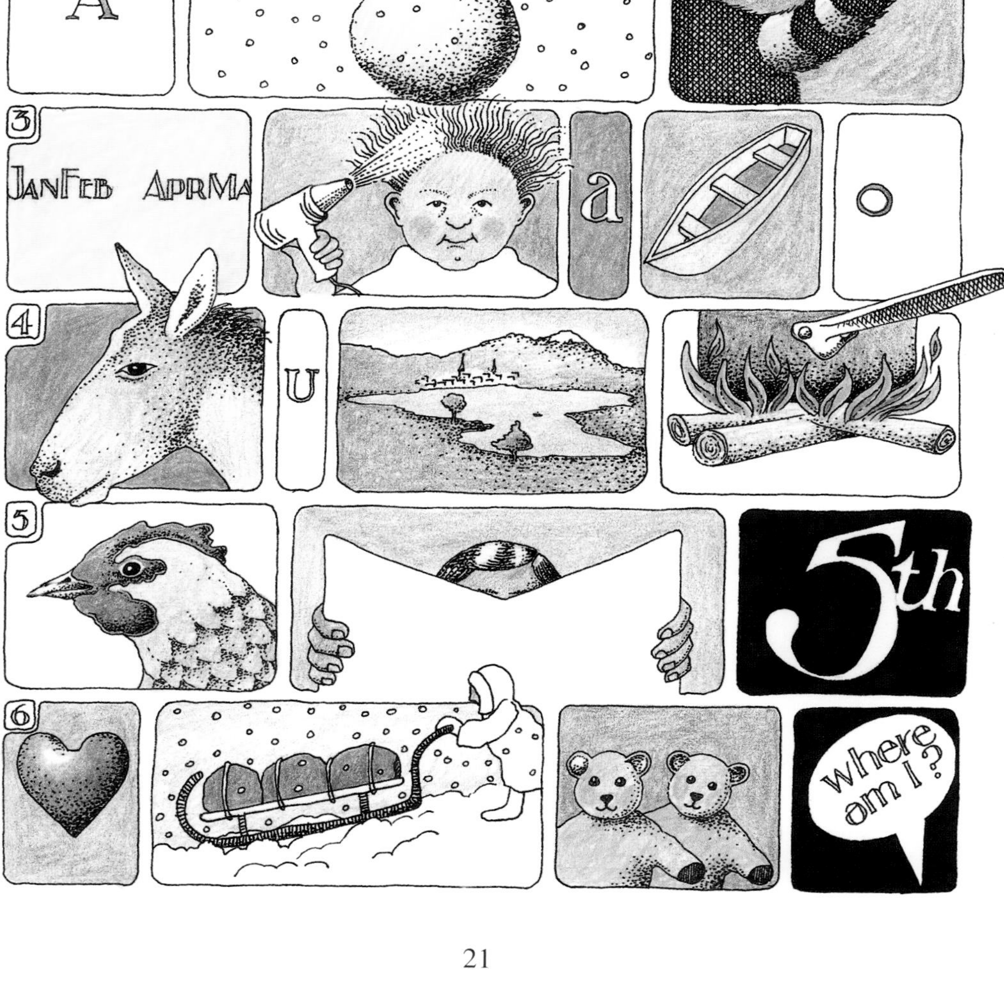

herbaceous border collie

jean paul goat (EA)

A Different Sunday

An eerie feeling met him at the altar:
what it was he never really knew.
He felt his need to make a sermon falte
he heard a whisper jump from pew to pew

It didn't seem the normal congregation:
he'd never seen those figures at the back.
And just before he started his oration
he clearly heard a tiny muffled quack.

ele mental

"We are not a moose."

SPOT THE FILM

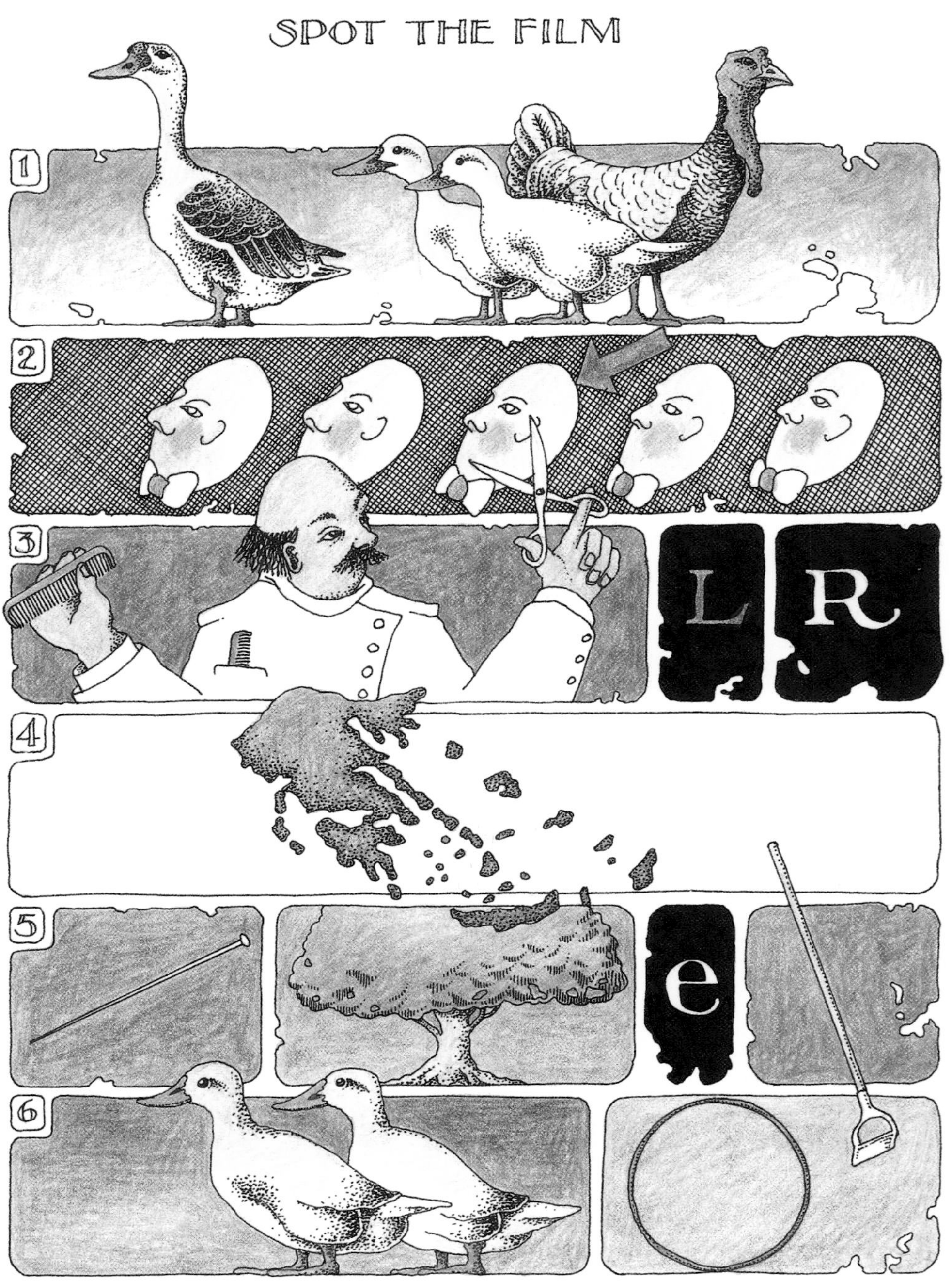

SPOT THE FILM

SPOT THE PLACE IN AUSTRALIA

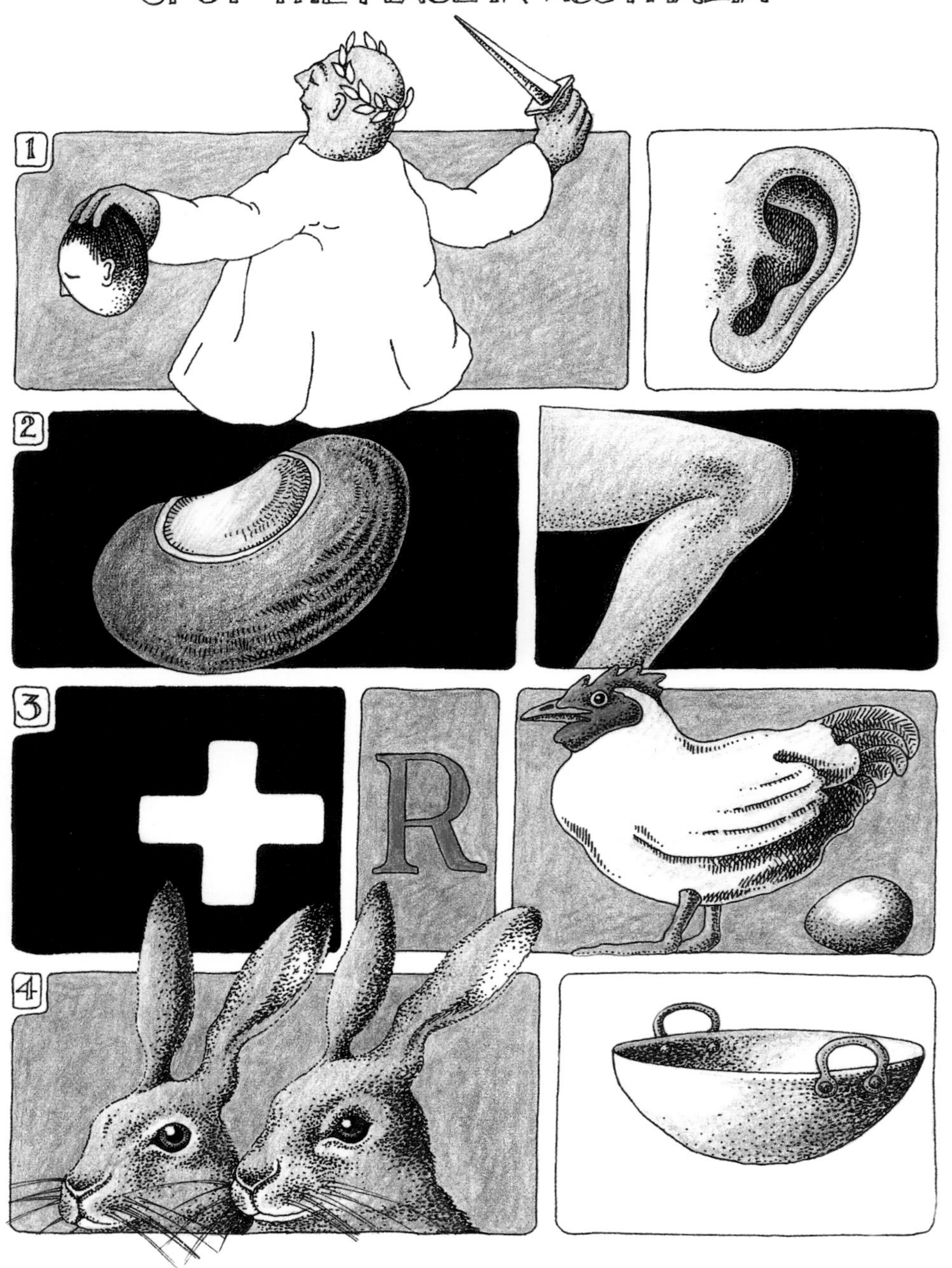

SPOT ANOTHER WINE

tess of the dormobiles

star sheep enterprise

SPOT THE AUTHOR

1

X

2

M

3

4

GRAHAM

5

6

SPOT THE LEGAL PROFESSION

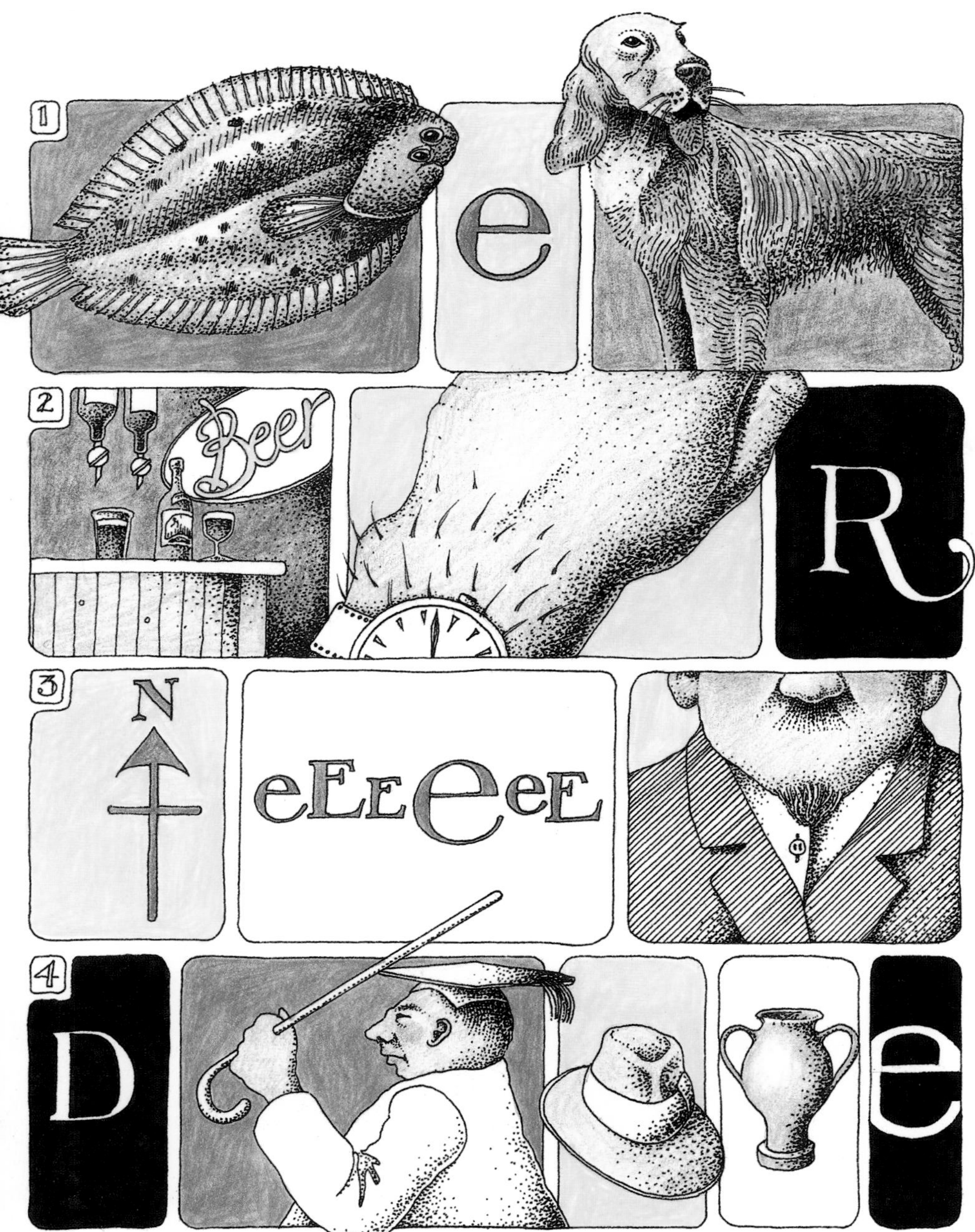

SPOT THE DIFFERENCE

GREY PLOVER GRAPE LOVER

you say potato
I say dauphinoise

Musicals we've never seen

by Gilbert & Sullivan

about cyclops

about a sweet shop

about skeletons in cupboards

Musicals we've never seen

...about the French

by
Robert Burns

about
mobile phones

about a greek poet
making tree-preservation
regulations

KING OF SHELLS

Rock of ages,
King of shells,
make your magic
cast your spells.

When the moon is in the east
call a doctor, call a priest.
They will make the spirits fly;
they can give the reason why
every creature, every thing
shields its eyes
before the King.

Could this thing that comes from Hades
be so bright, they should wear shades?

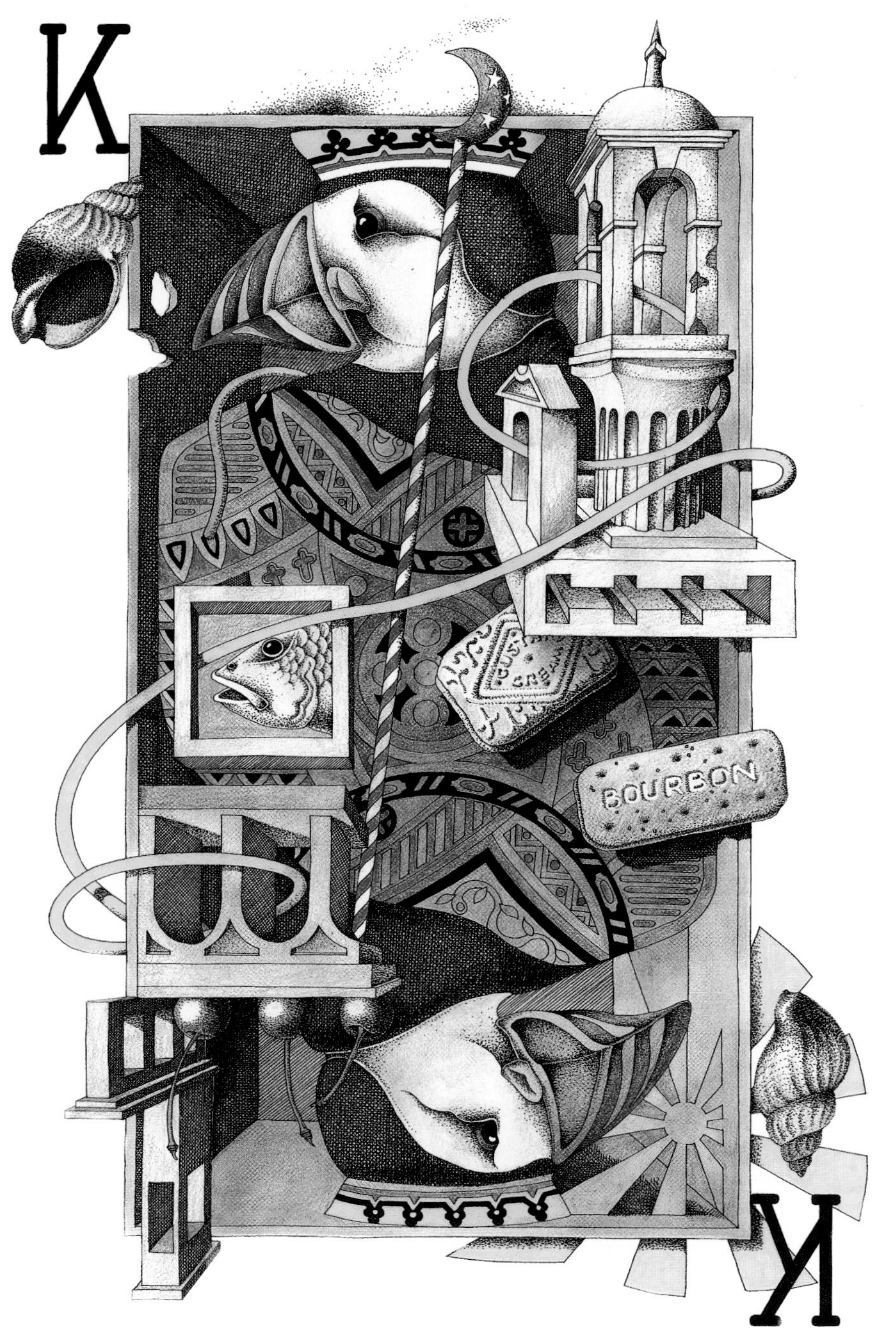
K
BOURBON

SPOT THE BRITISH POET

SPOT THE MUSICAL

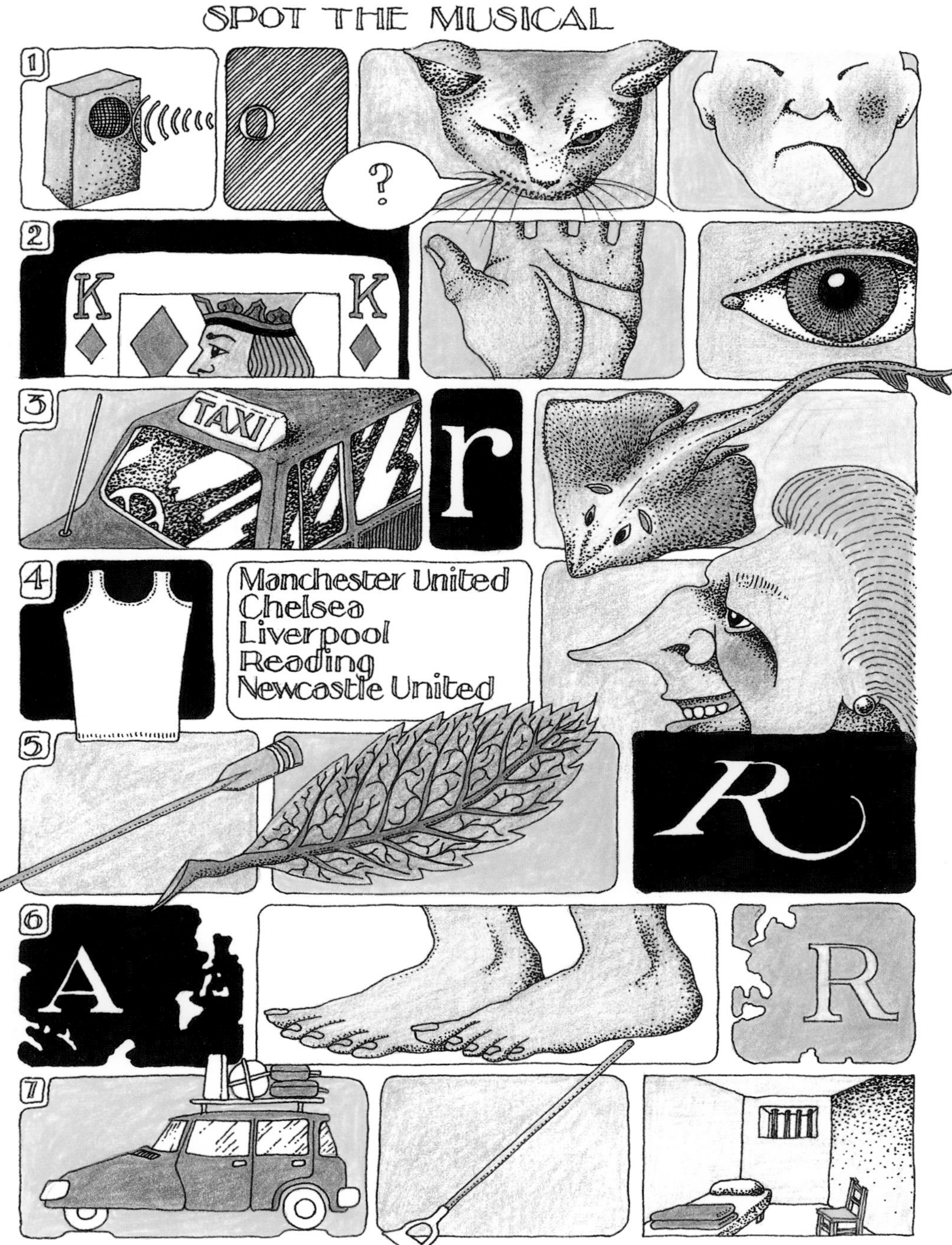

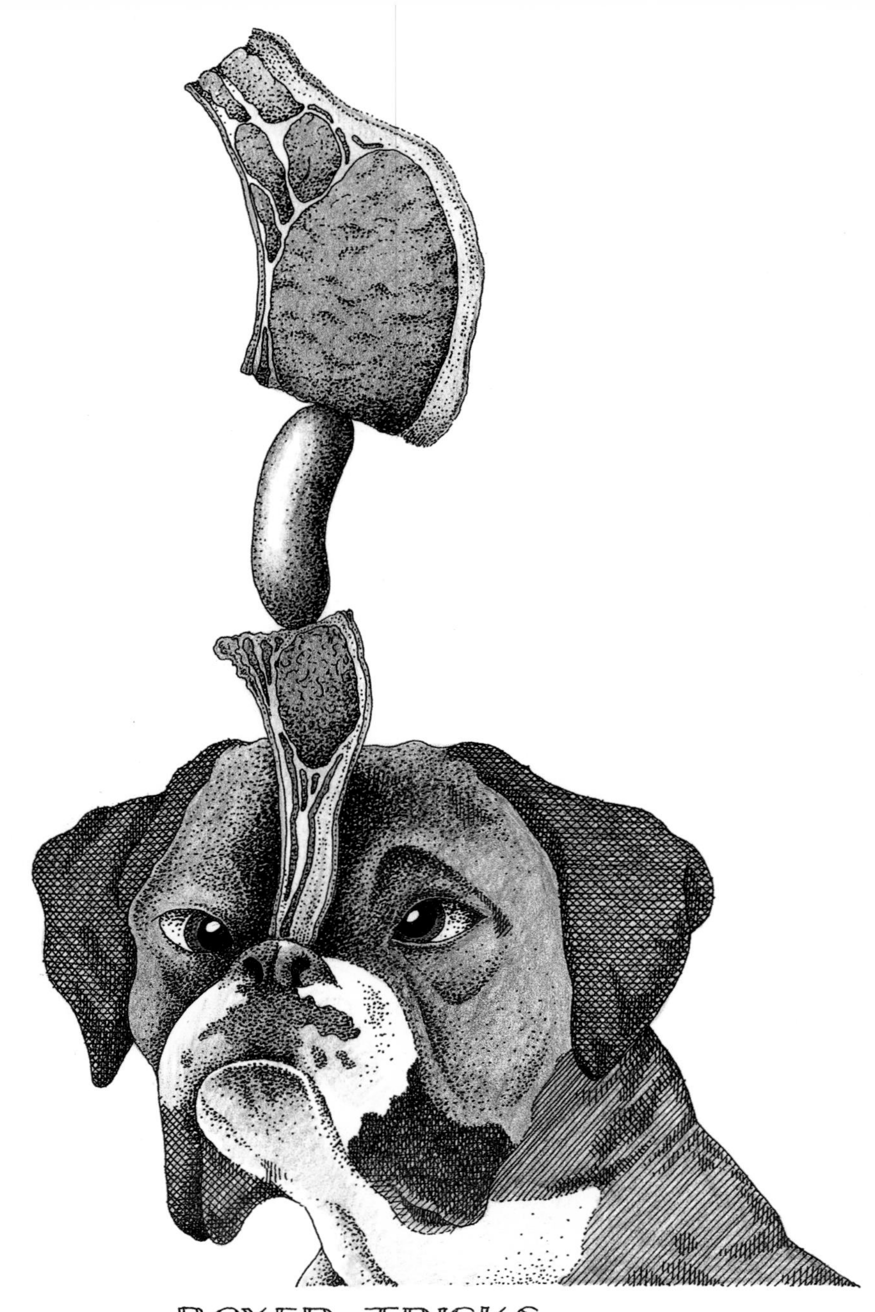

BOXER TRICKS

BEWARE: WEAPON OF MATHS DESTRUCTION

SPOT THE FLOWERS

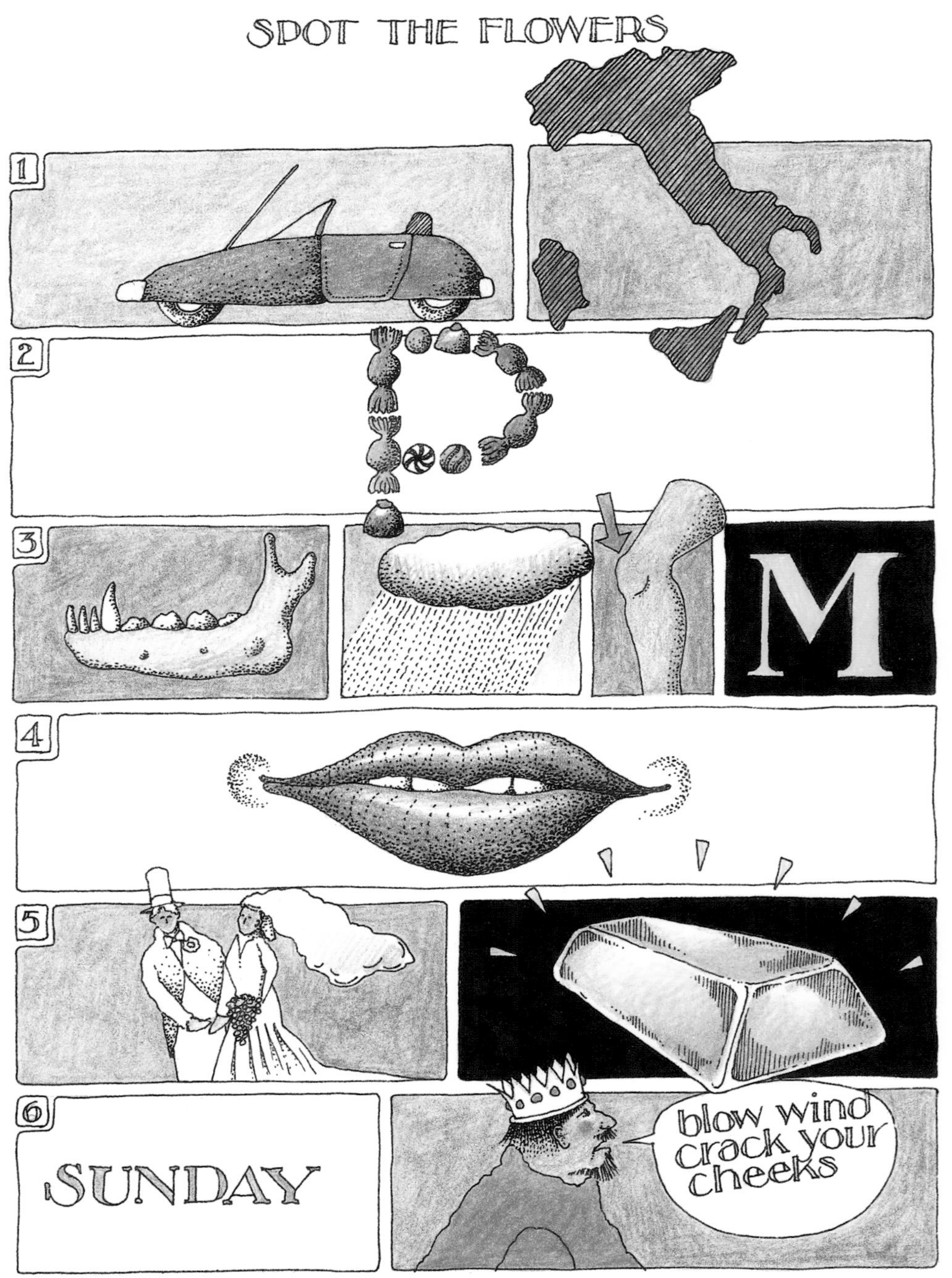

SPOT THE BRITISH CITY

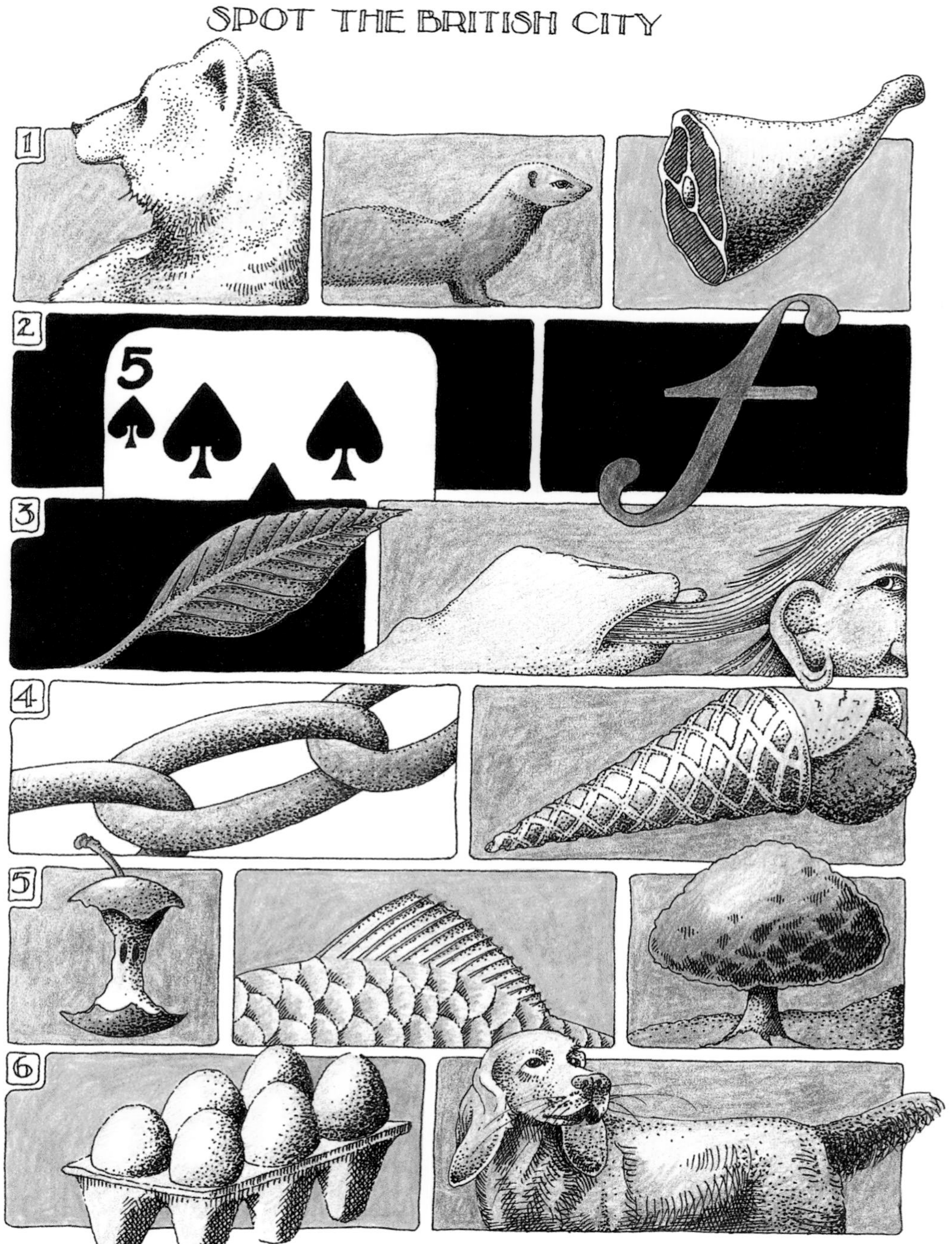

Answers Page

For the miserable sum of a fiver
made out to the Friends of the Earth
I'll help you become a survivor,
I'll send you solutions of worth.
The clues that I give are extensive
to make all the puzzles seem clearer.
(Predicting the future's expensive;
the meaning of life is much dearer).

o o o

So if you want to know the answers to the SPOT pages, make out a cheque for £5 to Friends of the Earth or send £5 or equivalent to the Simon Drew Gallery Foss Street Dartmouth Devon TQ6 9DR U.K. And if the answers annoy you, don't blame me.

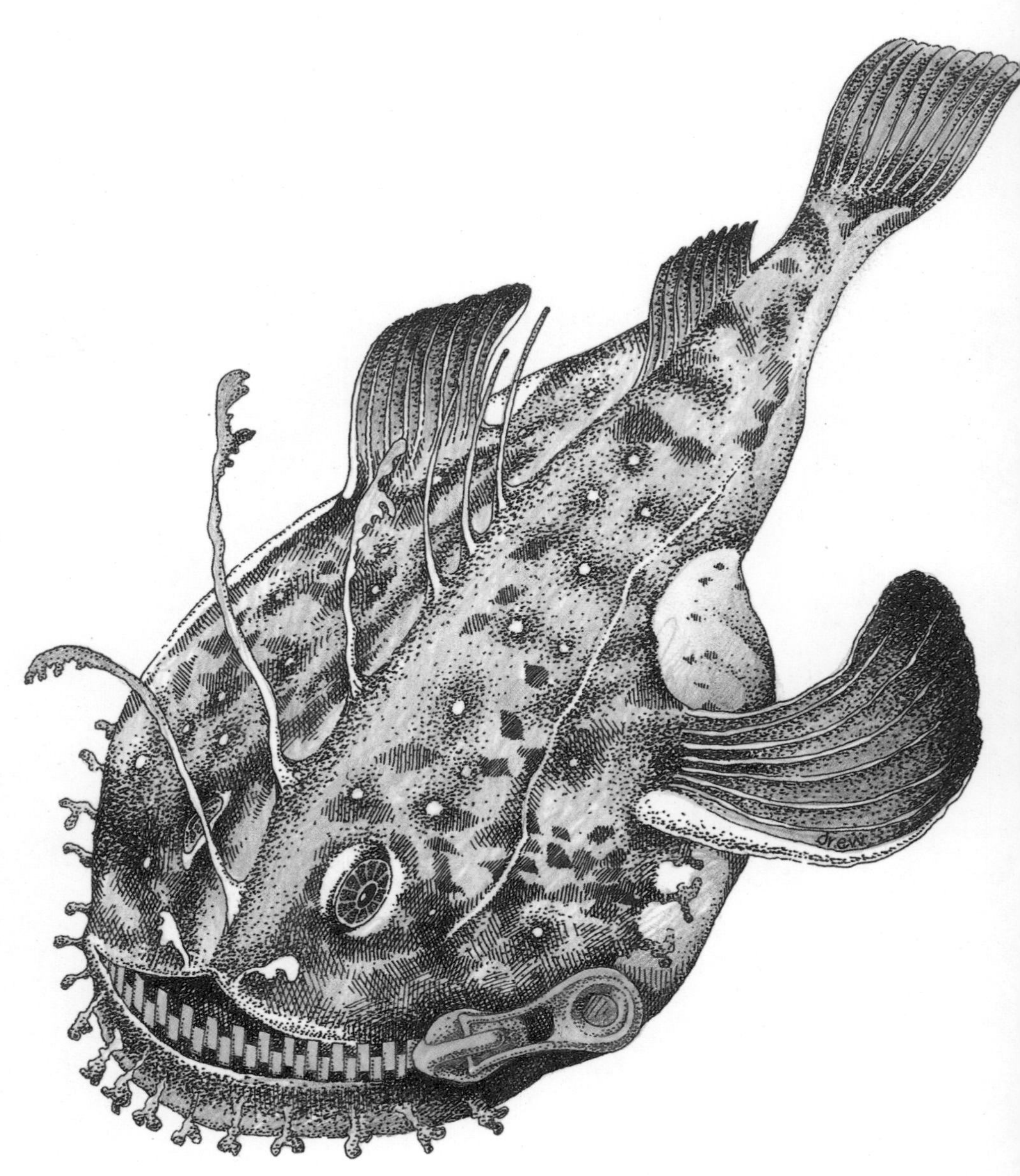

trappist monkfish